To _____

From _____

Date _____

Blessed
IS SHE

A GUIDED JOURNAL

NANCY TAYLOR

CHRISTIAN ART
PUBLISHERS

Published by Christian Art Publishers
PO Box 1599, Vereeniging, 1930, RSA

© 2021
First edition 2021

Designed by Christian Art Publishers

Cover designed by Christian Art Publishers
Images used under license from Shutterstock.com

Printed in China

ISBN 978-1-77637-023-8

Introduction

Do you consider yourself blessed? We often think of "blessing" in terms of the good things in life, but that's not how the Bible defines blessing. The title of this journal is taken from Luke 1:45, where Mary the mother of Jesus is called blessed because she believed God's promises. According to Scripture, blessing even comes in poverty and sorrow (Matthew 5:3-12). In short, blessing is the work of God in our lives. That means every one of us is blessed, because we have the promises of God to cling to and the assurance that He is working in our lives.

Yet all too often we miss the blessing because we fail to notice it. Mary trusted God's promises, but she also pondered God's works in her heart and thought about them often (Luke 2:19). She understood that the secret of living a blessed life is reflecting on what God is doing.

That's what this journal is all about. Each entry has a devotional thought, a verse, and a prompt to help you think about your life. As you work through the book, you'll be inspired to see God's providence in your past, ponder God's grace in your life right now, and look toward the future in faith. With each page you'll be encouraged to reflect on God's work in your life—blessings you're grateful for now and the ones you long for in the days to come.

"Blessed is she who has believed that the Lord would fulfill His promises to her!"

LUKE 1:45

Favorite
Christmas Gifts

Many mothers spend the better part of the year choosing their children's Christmas gifts, picking up things that make them say, "She would love this!" and then tucking them away in secret hiding spots until December. As you think back on all the gifts that showed you how much you were loved as a child, relive that joy as an expression of your heavenly Father's love for you.

List your favorite Christmas gifts from childhood.

Jesus replied, "If you only knew the gift God has for you and who you are speaking to, you would ask me, and I would give you living water." — JOHN 4:10

Favorite
Childhood Memories

Most of our days slip by almost unnoticed in the mundane dailiness of life. We do the next thing, we set our habits, we do what needs to be done. But every now and then something bursts through the ordinary and we remember it. Perhaps we were surprised by a special joy or were struck by a blessed gift straight from God. What were the sparkling days that have stuck with you through the years?

Reflect on your favorite memories from childhood.

Direct your children onto the right path, and when they are older, they will not leave it. — PROVERBS 22:6

Places that Inspire

Snow-capped mountains, sparkling in the sun and begging to be explored. The glistening lights of Paris, calling us to linger over a delicious meal and a good conversation. A cozy cabin in the wilderness, beckoning us to linger by the fire with a good book. What places have inspired and refreshed you, and whom did you share these moments with?

Describe the places that inspire you most. What makes them so great?

Then Jesus said, "Let's go off by ourselves to a quiet place and rest awhile."
— MARK 6:31

Favorite Memories
from the Past Year

At the turning of the calendar from one year to the next, whether it's the new year or our birthday or the start of a new school year, we often take stock of where we are and where we'd like to be. But perhaps best of all is to look back on the joyful moments from the previous year and thank God for them.

What are your favorite memories from the past year?

_____

_____

_____

_____

_____

_____

_____

_____

But then I recall all you have done, O Lᴏʀᴅ; I remember your wonderful deeds of long ago. — PSALM 77:11

Inspiring Words

A well-timed compliment does more than make us feel good; it makes us want to become a better person. It not only affirms who we are now, it inspires us to become the person we want to be in the future. And those positive messages stick with us for years, proving themselves true as we strive to fulfill them even more.

Write down the positive words that people have spoken over you, the gifts and strengths they have affirmed in you.

For we are God's masterpiece. He has created us anew in Christ Jesus, so we can do the good things he planned for us long ago. — EPHESIANS 2:10

Give thanks to the Lord.

PSALM 106:1

Favorite Books

One of my greatest joys in life is curling up with a good book and a warm cup of coffee, preferably with a pair of fuzzy slippers and a warm blanket. Not far behind is the joy of revisiting the old friends I've met in books many years ago. What books have stuck with you, and which ones might deserve a return visit in the months ahead?

List your favorite books.

All Scripture is inspired by God and is useful to teach us what is true and to make us realize what is wrong in our lives. It corrects us when we are wrong and teaches us to do what is right. — 2 TIMOTHY 3:16

Known For

My grandma was known for serving the best cookies for coffee time at church. My mom is known for her listening ear and words of wisdom. We're all known for things—small things like the way we put together an outfit, or bigger things like the circumstances that define our lives or the character traits and gifts that God is growing in us. What are the things people notice about you?

Reflect on some of the things you're known for.

_____

_____

_____

_____

_____

_____

_____

God has given each of you a gift from his great variety of spiritual gifts. Use them well to serve one another. — 1 PETER 4:10

Favorite Jobs

My first real job was as a janitor, cleaning dorm rooms at the local college during the summer. That wasn't my favorite job, though it did teach me about the value of hard work. Through the years I've worn many hats, some official and some not, some for pay and some for love. What jobs have you had that truly inspired you and brought you joy, and what did you love about them?

List your favorite jobs or tasks from the past.

Know the state of your flocks, and put your heart into caring for your herds.
— PROVERBS 27:23

Good Judgment

Children often make a snap judgment about a food they are offered, and sometimes down the road they discover they actually like it. We all do that from time to time. In fact, one mark of maturity is the ability to withhold judgment when faced with something new. What were some things you misjudged at first—and what are some new things or ideas you might need to give a chance to?

Write down the things or people you misjudged before you really got to know them.

_____

_____

_____

_____

_____

_____

_____

_____

Live in harmony with each other. Don't be too proud to enjoy the company of ordinary people. And don't think you know it all! — ROMANS 12:16

Favorite Places

I've found my happy place in a lot of different environments: camping on Prince Edward Island; exploring Dover Castle; looking out at the view from Table Mountain; walking on the nature trail near my home; sitting in the chair in my bedroom with my Bible open on my lap. Each of these places has been a gift to me, and I can return to them in my imagination when I am feeling overwhelmed or sad.

What are your favorite places, the environments that have made you feel happy and peaceful?

_____

_____

_____

_____

_____

_____

_____

Before the mountains were born, before you gave birth to the earth and the world, from beginning to end, you are God. — PSALM 90:2

Trust in the Lord with all your heart.

PROVERBS 3:5

Not So Important

Life has a way of changing our perspective. As we grow and change and gain distance from our past, we discover that some things were more important than we thought, while others were not as big of a deal as we made them out to be. Gaining perspective on our past enables us to predict which parts of our life now will be important in the future so we can live with our end in mind.

List the things you thought were important five or ten years ago that don't seem so important now.

_____

_____

_____

_____

_____

_____

_____

_____

_____

_____

Fix your thoughts on what is true, and honorable, and right, and pure, and lovely, and admirable. Think about things that are excellent and worthy of praise. — PHILIPPIANS 4:8

All the Difference

Life is, by its very nature, unpredictable. God rarely lets us see beyond the next step. But in hindsight we see how He was leading and directing each step to get us to where we are now. Take stock of all the ways God has illuminated your path as you list the little things you didn't expect to matter that turned out to make all the difference.

Which things that are important now did you not know would be important five or ten years ago?

Teach us to realize the brevity of life, so that we may grow in wisdom.
— PSALM 90:12

Belonging

It's been many years since I sat at my grandma's dinner table, but I still have a nostalgic longing for the feeling I had as we lingered after a meal, telling the old family stories. It wasn't just the people around the table that made it special, it was also the food and the beauty of the table setting, and I try to recreate that feeling for my guests whenever we have people in our home.

Write down the things that help you feel comfortable and accepted. How can you create that kind of environment for your loved ones?

Keep on loving each other as brothers and sisters. Don't forget to show hospitality to strangers, for some who have done this have entertained angels without realizing it! — HEBREWS 13:1-2

Money Matters

I've made some financial mistakes through the years—things I bought to solve a problem or fill a niche that turned out to never be quite right. Some of my mistakes were funny, some stung a bit, but all of them taught me important lessons about financial planning and patience. What financial mistakes have you made, and what can you learn from them?

Which things have you bought that you later regretted? Does this tell you anything about how you could spend your money better?

God will generously provide all you need. Then you will always have everything you need and plenty left over to share with others. — 2 CORINTHIANS 9:8

Sharing a Meal

Maybe it was a picnic with your new love. Maybe it was a birthday when you were a child. Or maybe it was your last meal with a grandparent. Think back on a meal with your mother, with your sister, with a good friend, with your beloved—cherish it and resolve to make a special meal this week for someone you care about.

Describe the best meal you've shared with a loved one—what did you eat? What was the environment like? What made it special? Then plan a special meal to share with someone this week.

_____

_____

_____

_____

_____

_____

_____

_____

"Look! I stand at the door and knock. If you hear my voice and open the door, I will come in, and we will share a meal together as friends."
— REVELATION 3:20

Cast
your cares
on the
Lord.

PSALM 55:22

Needless Worry

Cancer, car crashes, missed deadlines, house fires, Alzheimer's—the list of what-ifs that run through our minds and cause us to lose sleep is endless. Most of those things will never happen, and worrying about them doesn't keep them from happening anyway. And yet, if we let our minds wander, they often travel down the familiar paths of worry. Name them, and then let them go.

Reflect on the things that you used to worry about that never happened. What does that tell you about your current anxieties?

When doubts filled my mind, your comfort gave me renewed hope and cheer.
— PSALM 94:19

Accomplishments

I've never been much of a runner, or even an avid exerciser, but one year for some inexplicable reason I signed up to run a half-marathon. My feeling of triumph at the end of the race had nothing to do with my time, or even any positive effects on my body. My success lay in the fact that I had done something I never thought I could.

Write down some things you didn't think you could do, but then you did!

My help comes from the LORD, who made heaven and earth! — PSALM 121:2

God Moments

The course of life often takes unexpected turns down unwanted paths. We find ourselves far from where we wanted to be, with no way to get back to where we were. But if we look closely, we will find that God has been preparing us for this moment and comforting us in it. Look for those "God moments" and be reminded that He is near to the brokenhearted.

List the ways God has comforted you in your heartaches over the past year.

_____

_____

_____

_____

_____

_____

_____

_____

Even when I walk through the darkest valley, I will not be afraid, for you are close beside me. Your rod and your staff protect and comfort me.
— PSALM 23:4

Thankful for These

We all have people who showed us the path of life and taught us how to follow Jesus. Maybe it was your third-grade Sunday school teacher. Perhaps it was the pastor who preached the Word, in season and out of season. Or maybe it was a small group leader, a trusted friend, or a beloved parent. Whatever their name, however long ago they influenced you, they are worth remembering and thanking God for.

Who has helped you most in your walk with the Lord? Write them a note of gratitude.

I always thank my God for you and for the gracious gifts he has given you, now that you belong to Christ Jesus. — 1 CORINTHIANS 1:4

Growth through Trials

Nietzsche said, "Whatever doesn't kill you makes you stronger." Taken to the extreme, we may argue with the sentiment. But there is some truth to the idea that experiencing difficulties makes us better people. The entire weight-lifting industry is built on this premise, and the Bible bears witness to it. God uses trials to make us mature and complete, fashioning us into the people He is calling us to be.

Which challenges has God used to make you the person He wants you to be?

_____

_____

_____

_____

_____

_____

_____

Dear brothers and sisters, when troubles of any kind come your way, consider it an opportunity for great joy. For you know that when your faith is tested, your endurance has a chance to grow. So let it grow, for when your endurance is fully developed, you will be perfect and complete, needing nothing. — JAMES 1:2-4

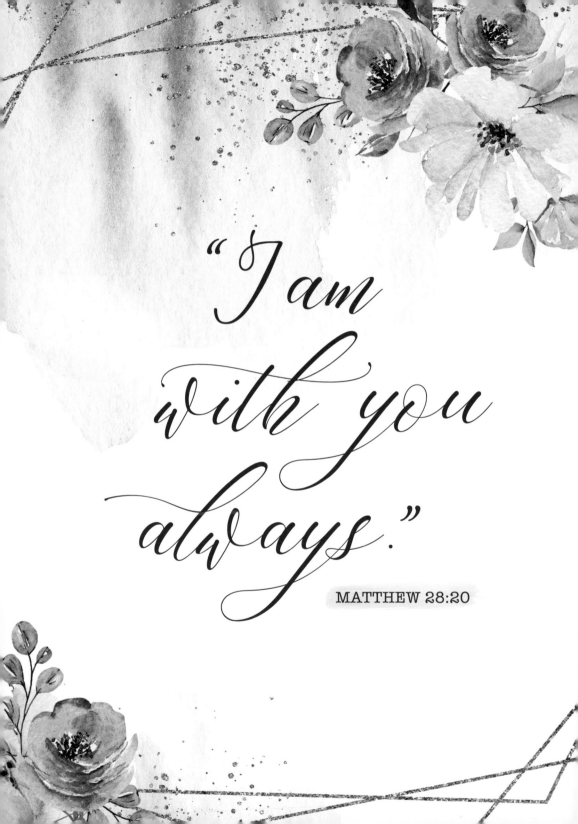

"I am
with you
always."

MATTHEW 28:20

Not Afraid
Anymore

Nineteen million people in the United States suffer from phobias—intense, irrational fears. Phobia or not, all of us can find plenty of things to fear, whether it's a legitimate fear about something that is likely to happen or an unfounded fear of something that has a one-in-a-million chance of coming to pass. Sometimes it's helpful to look back on all the fears we've conquered to help us face the ones we are still struggling to overcome.

List some things you used to be afraid of but aren't anymore.

_____

_____

_____

_____

_____

_____

_____

_____

So be strong and courageous! Do not be afraid and do not panic before them. For the LORD your God will personally go ahead of you. He will neither fail you nor abandon you. — DEUTERONOMY 31:6

Old Friends

Many of the things we love in adulthood are born out of happy childhood memories, and the sweetest friendships are often those we have had the longest. There's just something about the innocence of childhood that brings a smile to your face. Spend a few minutes walking down memory lane and revisit your childhood haunts with old friends in your mind's eye.

Who were your friends in childhood, and what fun things did you do together?

There are "friends" who destroy each other, but a real friend sticks closer than a brother. — PROVERBS 18:24

Dressed for Success

My light blue corduroy pants and the matching plaid shirt with a shiny metallic thread woven through it filled my nine-year-old soul with delight. The fancy dress my mother made for my senior prom made me feel beautiful. The right clothing item at the right moment can change our mood, boost our confidence, and help us get the job we want.

Describe or draw your favorite clothing item—why was it special to you?

Clothe yourselves . . . with the beauty that comes from within, the unfading beauty of a gentle and quiet spirit, which is so precious to God. — 1 PETER 3:4

Memories of Mom

I think every mom out there has a "thing," that special talent she brings to her mothering. For some it's the ability to throw a spectacular party. For others it's the way they draw their children's friends in and offer wise counsel. Still others demonstrate the ability to use their talents in the workplace while caring for their children. As you think back on your childhood, what was your mom's "thing"?

List your favorite memories of your mother.

_____

_____

_____

_____

_____

_____

_____

_____

_____

_____

Her children stand and bless her. Her husband praises her: "There are many virtuous and capable women in the world, but you surpass them all!"
— PROVERBS 31:28-29

Memories of Dad

God gives us earthly fathers to show us what our heavenly Father's love is like—at once tender and strong, protector and friend. Of course, not every earthly father does a good job of that, and all earthly fathers disappoint us sometimes. Still, looking back on all our earthly fathers did imperfectly can remind us of God's perfect love.

Reflect on your favorite memories of your father.

The LORD is like a father to his children, tender and compassionate to those who fear him. — PSALM 103:13

His
mercies
are new
every
morning.

LAMENTATIONS 3:22-23

Grateful & Blessed

Right now I'm in my favorite writing chair, in the corner of my bedroom, looking out of the window at the street in front of our house. Next to me is a basket with my Bible, journal, and collection of colored pens. From this vantage point I see so many reminders of God's faithful provision and creativity, and it encourages me to respond to Him in grateful praise.

List the things you see right now, wherever you are sitting, that you are thankful for.

_____

_____

_____

_____

_____

_____

_____

_____

Be thankful in all circumstances, for this is God's will for you who belong to Christ Jesus. — 1 THESSALONIANS 5:18

Good Gifts

Yesterday I took a long walk with a friend. Last night I shared a casual pizza dinner with my family and we talked about our day. A few days ago I received a card from a friend, just when I needed some encouragement. Each of us receives little gifts like this, and if we pay attention to them we will see that they are reminders of God's loving care for us.

Which gifts has God given you this week that remind you of His love?

_____

_____

_____

_____

_____

_____

_____

_____

Whatever is good and perfect is a gift coming down to us from God our Father, who created all the lights in the heavens. He never changes or casts a shifting shadow. — JAMES 1:17

Unexpected Paths

Your five- or ten-year plan probably didn't work out quite the way you thought it would. Most of us either fail to meet our goals or are faced with circumstances that fail us. Yet in hindsight, we find that God's ways are actually better than our ways. Even the difficulties that cause us to grow turn out to be worth the cost.

List the ways your life has turned out different than you expected—and why you think God has put you on that path.

_"For I know the plans I have for you," says the L_ord_. "They are plans for good and not for disaster, to give you a future and a hope." — JEREMIAH 29:11_

Feeling Alive

Is it the smell of salty, fresh air and the feeling of sand between your toes? Is it the scent of freshly-baked bread that you made from scratch to share with a friend? Maybe it's a long conversation with someone you love. We all have things that make us feel alive, and listing them can remind us to seek out more of them.

Write down the things, experiences, and people that help you feel alive.

He alone is your God, the only one who is worthy of your praise, the one who has done these mighty miracles that you have seen with your own eyes.
— DEUTERONOMY 10:21

Gift of Peace

God offers us peace that rises above our circumstances. Even in the face of suffering and death, He gives us sweet times of peace and refreshment deep in our souls. The storms of life can't touch us when we are hiding ourselves in Him. He also gives us practical tools—daily life rhythms that we can use to reorient ourselves to the hope we have in Him.

What things bring you peace?

_____

_____

_____

_____

_____

_____

_____

_____

_____

"I am leaving you with a gift—peace of mind and heart. And the peace I give is a gift the world cannot give. So don't be troubled or afraid." — JOHN 14:27

Rejoice in the Lord.

PHILIPPIANS 4:4

Surprise Opportunities

Nothing takes God by surprise—not the change in our circumstances or the loss of a job or the sudden death of a loved one. Nonetheless, we are often surprised by God. He brings things into our lives that are far above what we could have asked or imagined, and it is these surprise opportunities that turn out to be the best gifts of all.

Which opportunities has God given you that you never would have expected?

_____

_____

_____

_____

_____

_____

_____

Make the most of every opportunity in these evil days. Don't act thoughtlessly, but understand what the Lord wants you to do. — EPHESIANS 5:16-17

Seasons of Life

God created the world with seasons for the nourishment and delight of His creatures. There is a time for every purpose under heaven—both the seasons of nature and the seasons of our lives. Appreciating where we are, with all of its transitions and joys and challenges, is part of developing a heart of gratitude for all of God's blessings.

What are your favorite things about the season you are in (either the season of the year or the season of your life)?

For everything there is a season, a time for every activity under heaven.
— ECCLESIASTES 3:1

Abundant Joy

Throughout Scripture there is a theme of abundant joy that comes not from circumstances, but from intimacy with the Lord. In addition to that deep joy, God "richly gives us all we need for our enjoyment" (1 Timothy 6:17). He established feasts and celebrations and simple daily pleasures to delight us, and it gives God pleasure when we enjoy the gifts He gives.

Write down some things that bring you joy.

This is the day the LORD has made. We will rejoice and be glad in it.
— PSALM 118:24

A Beautiful *World*

There's nothing quite as delightful as a campfire on a crisp fall evening, a morning spent on the water in a boat, or a long walk on a summer afternoon. God created a beautiful world that displays His glory. Enjoying God's creation, in all of its vast beauty and lush variety, is one way we can connect with God our Creator.

What are your favorite things to do outside?

For ever since the world was created, people have seen the earth and sky. Through everything God made, they can clearly see his invisible qualities— his eternal power and divine nature. — ROMANS 1:20

Favorite Songs

When I was in junior high it was the latest hit by a popular Christian artist. Now it runs more along the lines of Beethoven or a particular choral arrangement of a beloved hymn. Music, in all its vast array, moves us like nothing else. It helps us express sorrow too deep for words and provides a soundtrack to the daily celebrations of our lives.

List your favorite songs.

_____

_____

_____

_____

_____

_____

_____

_____

_____

_____

Come, let us sing to the LORD! Let us shout joyfully to the Rock of our salvation.
— PSALM 95:1

We love because He first loved us.

1 JOHN 4:19

Gentle Words

Words have the power to build up or tear down, to give life or bring destruction. Proverbs tells us that "the words of the godly are a life-giving fountain" (Proverbs 10:11). One of the secrets to learning how to speak life-giving words is paying attention to the words others speak that encourage us. The art of encouragement can be learned through repetition and practice.

List the things people have said to you that have really encouraged you. Whom could you encourage today with a similar word?

Gentle words are a tree of life. — PROVERBS 15:4

Taking a Break

The greatest gift you can give to a busy mother or an overworked executive is a day off—a few hours with no deadlines, no demands, no emails to answer. The funny thing is, sometimes when we do find ourselves with a few hours off we can't figure out what we want to do. Here's your chance to plan ahead for your next day off.

What things do you most love to do?

_____

_____

_____

_____

_____

_____

_____

_____

_____

A cheerful heart is good medicine, but a broken spirit saps a person's strength.
— PROVERBS 17:22

A Heart of *Worship*

The ruins of a medieval cathedral. A pine forest in the Northwoods of Wisconsin. An empty beach at sunrise. A church service shared with family and friends. All of these have been houses of worship for me at different times. Where does your heart naturally start to worship, just because of the surroundings?

Write down the times and places when you find it easy to worship God. What fosters a heart of worship in you?

_____

_____

_____

_____

_____

_____

_____

_____

Come, let us worship and bow down. Let us kneel before the LORD our maker. — PSALM 95:6

Speaking Love

A wise spouse learns how to speak their beloved's love language, whether it is acts of service or words of affirmation or physical touch or time spent together that speaks most loudly to their heart. Likewise, a good friend will work at expressing love to their friends in a variety of ways. How wide is your love vocabulary, and how could you expand it even more?

Write down the things that make you feel loved. How can you do those things for someone this week?

There is no greater love than to lay down one's life for one's friends.
— JOHN 15:13

God's Faithfulness

The book of Lamentations tells us that God's mercies are fresh each morning and His faithfulness never ends (3:22-23). Sometimes in the bustle of life it's easy to lose sight of God's faithfulness. Take a long look back at the significant events in your life and see how God used people and experiences to guide you, and then look at the last few days and think about how He has shown you His love.

List some of the ways God has been faithful to you.

Let all that I am praise the LORD; may I never forget the good things he does for me. — PSALM 103:2

He fills my
life with
good
things.

PSALM 103:5

Working with Joy

Some of the things we do each day just have to get done, whether we like them or not—things like taking out the trash or cleaning the bathroom or doing the dishes. But many of our work tasks can and should give us joy, if we can just learn to savor them and appreciate the gifts that they are.

What are your favorite jobs right now—what work gives you joy and purpose?

_____

_____

_____

_____

_____

_____

_____

_____

_____

Work willingly at whatever you do, as though you were working for the Lord rather than for people. — COLOSSIANS 3:23

Great Blessings

Each stage of life brings its share of joy as well as its moments of sorrow. There is blessing to be found wherever we are. Appreciating and giving thanks for the unique blessings each season of life offers can help us live a life of gratitude and point us back to the One who makes everything beautiful in its time (Ecclesiastes 3:11).

What are your greatest blessings at this stage of life?

How great is the goodness you have stored up for those who fear you. You lavish it on those who come to you for protection, blessing them before the watching world. — PSALM 31:19

Glorious Beauty

Sometimes beauty is easy to see—a sunset at the beach or the blush on a peach-colored rose or a baby's first smiles. Other times we might have to look for it, especially at those times when life is hard. But it's always there. God displays His glory through beauties big and small, and He is always glorious.

Describe moments of beauty you've experienced in the past week.

The heavens proclaim the glory of God. The skies display his craftsmanship.
— PSALM 19:1

No Place like *Home*

The phrase "home is where the heart is" was coined for a reason. Our houses are more than the place we lay our head, they are the place where we experience peace, comfort, and love. Every now and then it's nice to step back, clear away the clutter of the everyday, and appreciate all the things we love about our home.

What is your favorite space in your house? Write down the things you love about it and what you enjoy doing there.

_____

_____

_____

_____

_____

_____

_____

_____

"Anyone who listens to my teaching and follows it is wise, like a person who builds a house on solid rock." — MATTHEW 7:24

Expressions of *Love*

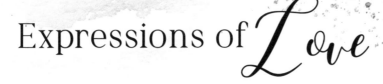

Love expressed only in words is not love at all. Actions prove the authenticity and depth of our love. But sometimes we forget that. We get so busy that we struggle to both give and receive love. When we find ourselves in that spot, feeling unloved and unloving, it's good to be reminded of all the ways people have shown love to us.

List the people who have shown kindness to you this week and the things they did for you.

Dear children, let's not merely say that we love each other; let us show the truth by our actions. — 1 JOHN 3:18

"Be still,
and know
that
I am God."

PSALM 46:10

Keep Learning

The Bible encourages us to keep learning and growing, to refuse to stay where we are but instead lean deeper and more fully into all God wants to teach us. What habits are helping you continue to learn? How can you encourage a flourishing life of the mind for yourself and your loved ones?

Write down the things you learned this week.

_____

_____

_____

_____

_____

_____

_____

_____

_____

Fear of the LORD is the foundation of true knowledge, but fools despise wisdom and discipline. — PROVERBS 1:7

Taste and See

Maybe you're a gourmet cook, or maybe comfort food is more your style. Maybe you add chili pepper seasoning to everything, or maybe your palate can't handle anything spicy. Whatever your personal tastes, food is intended to bring joy as well as nourishment. That's why God encourages us to taste His goodness, not just think about it. What are your favorite flavors?

List the best things you've ever tasted.

_____

_____

_____

_____

_____

_____

_____

_____

_____

_____

_____

Taste and see that the LORD is good. Oh, the joys of those who take refuge in him! — PSALM 34:8

A Sense of *Touch*

God created our senses so that we could fully experience His magnificent creation. Our sense of touch is what connects us to the world around us and to one another. Filling our homes and our lives with textures and experiences that enhance our joy and restore our souls through the sense of touch can help us worship God more freely.

What are some things you touched this week that brought you comfort or joy?

_____

_____

_____

_____

_____

_____

_____

_____

We proclaim to you the one who existed from the beginning, whom we have heard and seen. We saw him with our own eyes and touched him with our own hands. He is the Word of life. — 1 JOHN 1:1

Favorite Hobbies

It is a blessing and a joy to discover a new hobby—that's why adult education classes are so popular. Different seasons of life offer different opportunities and amounts of time to pursue our hobbies, but keeping a list of things we enjoy and want to pursue will help us make the most of whatever time we have available.

What are your favorite hobbies?

_____

_____

_____

_____

_____

_____

_____

_____

May he grant your heart's desires and make all your plans succeed.
— PSALM 20:4

Favorite Bible Verses

God's Word is unlike any other book. It is living and active (Hebrews 4:12), which means it can speak to us in a unique way as the Holy Spirit breathes it afresh into our soul. Verses we've read hundreds of times before can suddenly jump off the page at the moment we need to hear them.

List the Bible verses that have meant a lot to you and the reason they stand out.

The grass withers and the flowers fade, but the word of our God stands forever.
— ISAIAH 40:8

My hope comes from Him.

PSALM 62:5

Letting Go

We live in an era of outrage and moral indignation. People are looking for reasons to be the victim or causes to champion on social media. It's easy to get so busy being angry that we forget how to forgive. Listing the things that bother us can help us realize which of our causes are more about our own pride than they are about doing what's right.

What are some things you're offended by that you need to let go of?

_____

_____

_____

_____

_____

_____

_____

_____

Make allowance for each other's faults, and forgive anyone who offends you.
Remember, the Lord forgave you, so you must forgive others.
— COLOSSIANS 3:13

Hope & Healing

There are plenty of things we are outraged about but shouldn't be. It's good to let go of those. But there are some things that are genuine injustices, things that grieve the heart of God. Those are causes that we should be concerned about, and there are probably a few that God is calling you to personally engage with.

What are some injustices you see that really touch your heart? What part might God have for you in bringing hope and healing?

_____

_____

_____

_____

_____

_____

_____

_____

_____

_____

The Lord has told you what is good, and this is what he requires of you:
to do what is right, to love mercy, and to walk humbly with your God.
— MICAH 6:8

Obeying God's Will

There are times we wonder what God wants us to do. We search for guidance and wish we could hear God's voice audibly so we could better discern His will. But other times—probably more often than we want to admit—we do know what we should do, we just don't want to do it. Here is a space to admit the places you're resisting God's will.

List some things you know God wants you to do but you've been resisting. Ask Him to help you obey.

"If you love me, obey my commandments." — JOHN 14:15

Of Eternal Value

A devastating diagnosis or sudden tragedy causes us to take stock of our lives. We are faced with our mortality, and it gives us a fresh perspective on what's truly important. Suddenly we realize that much of what we do each day has no eternal value. How much better it would be to consider what's important before we're faced with a crisis and prioritize the things that have lasting value.

Write down the things you will want to have done when you look back over your life. Are you making time for those things?

Seek the Kingdom of God above all else, and live righteously, and he will give you everything you need. — MATTHEW 6:33

Healthy Relationships

A good relationship starts with living out God's commands to put others first and treat them the way we want to be treated—to love in the same way we are loved by Christ. But sometimes the best way to know what makes for a healthy relationship is to observe one up close so we can see how God's standards are played out in real life.

List the trademarks of a healthy relationship. How can you foster those characteristics in your relationships this week?

Share each other's burdens, and in this way obey the law of Christ.
— GALATIANS 6:2

Stand firm in the faith. Be courageous. Be strong.

1 CORINTHIANS 16:13

Deep Longings

Whether it's the traditional pickles and ice cream during a pregnancy, mom's casserole after a hard week, or a chocolate shake on a hot summer afternoon, we all know what it is to crave. If we pay attention, we will also notice that we have deeper hungers—for friendship or encouragement or forgiveness. The good news is, every one of those deep longings can be satisfied in Christ.

What are you hungry for? What is your deepest longing right now?

_____

_____

_____

_____

_____

_____

_____

As the deer longs for streams of water, so I long for You, O God. — PSALM 42:1

Saying No

It's often easier to say yes than to say no. We hate to let people down, and many of the opportunities in front of us are good things we want to say yes to. The problem comes when we say yes to everything, and we eventually come up against our limitations. If we try to do it all, we will end up doing nothing well.

Think about the things you know you need to say no to—and make an exit strategy you will put in place.

_____

_____

_____

_____

_____

_____

_____

_____

_____

_____

_____

I will bless the Lᴏʀᴅ who guides me; even at night my heart instructs me.
— PSALM 16:7

Saying Yes

In addition to figuring out what we should say no to, we also need to have the courage and discipline to say yes to the right things. Whether it's Bible study, investing in discipleship, or an opportunity to serve at our church or lead a ministry, there are many things we can say yes to that will have eternal value for ourselves and those around us.

Which opportunities for spiritual growth and service has God put in your path right now? Journal about ways you can maximize those opportunities in the weeks ahead.

Let's not get tired of doing what is good. At just the right time we will reap a harvest of blessing if we don't give up. — GALATIANS 6:9

Distractions

Some days I feel like my life is made up of distractions. My children need a ride somewhere. My boss needs me to drop everything and work on something. A friend calls and needs to talk. Those things are often the things that should be my priorities. More insidious—and more dangerous—are the distractions I make for myself when I waste my time and attention on lesser things instead of spending it on Jesus.

Which things are keeping you from a deeper walk with Jesus?

_____

_____

_____

_____

_____

Therefore, since we are surrounded by such a huge crowd of witnesses to the life of faith, let us strip off every weight that slows us down, especially the sin that so easily trips us up. And let us run with endurance the race God has set before us. — HEBREWS 12:1

Additions

It's easy to identify the things we need to cut out of our lives—distractions and sins that keep us from living the life God wants for us. Slightly more difficult is to figure out what things we want to add. Use this space to brainstorm. Set aside the time or financial barriers that might prevent you from actually doing these things and dream a little.

List the things you want to add to your life.

_____

_____

_____

_____

_____

_____

_____

_____

_____

Supplement your faith with a generous provision of moral excellence, and moral excellence with knowledge, and knowledge with self-control, and self-control with patient endurance, and patient endurance with godliness, and godliness with brotherly affection, and brotherly affection with love for everyone. — 2 PETER 1:5-7

Walk by faith, not by sight.

2 CORINTHIANS 5:7

Being Generous

Generosity breeds generosity. The more we give, the more we want to give. I think sometimes we fail to give simply because we don't have a vision for all the good we could do with the resources God has given us. Everything we have is from God, and it is our responsibility to be good stewards of the gifts we've been given.

List some things you'd like to give to—organizations or causes that are close to your heart. And then make a plan for doing so.

_____

_____

_____

_____

_____

_____

_____

Don't give reluctantly or in response to pressure. "For God loves a person who gives cheerfully." — 2 CORINTHIANS 9:7

Creatively Designed

God is first a Creator—that is the first thing we see Him doing in the Bible. As people made in His image, we are creators as well. And our creative endeavors can be done as an act of worship. So whether you are a painter or a crafter or a tinkerer, figure out how you can reflect the creativity of your Creator.

List some things you'd like to create in the next year.

Every house has a builder, but the one who built everything is God.
— HEBREWS 3:4

Living in Color

Golden-yellow. Calming cerulean. Lovely lavender. Bold red. Refreshing orange. God created the full spectrum of colors to make the world a beautiful place and to express His glory in all its radiance. We can use those same colors to understand and express ourselves in new ways.

If your life right now was a color, what color would it be and why? What color do you want it to be and why?

_____

_____

_____

_____

_____

_____

_____

The one sitting on the throne was as brilliant as gemstones—like jasper and carnelian. And the glow of an emerald circled his throne like a rainbow.
— REVELATION 4:3

True Rest

God designed us for rest. In fact, Sabbath rest is commanded as both an imitation of God's example and a sign of His covenant love (Exodus 31:16-17). But sometimes we waste our rest time or fail to truly rest because we don't have a plan. Think about what rejuvenates you and then find a way to incorporate more relaxation into your life.

Think about the things you would do if you were given a free day with no responsibilities. Choose one or two of these things to do this week.

_____

_____

_____

_____

_____

_____

_____

_____

Then Jesus said, "Come to me, all of you who are weary and carry heavy burdens, and I will give you rest." — MATTHEW 11:28

Healthy Habits

Research shows that when we find an exercise regimen we enjoy and create concrete goals, we are more likely to get in shape and stay in shape. Likewise, the more we eat healthy foods, the more we begin to crave them. Here's your chance to come up with a plan for a better you—body, mind, and spirit.

Write down the healthy habits that make you feel strong and energized.

Physical training is good, but training for godliness is much better, promising benefits in this life and in the life to come. —1 TIMOTHY 4:8

" *My grace is all you need.* "

2 CORINTHIANS 12:9

Holiday Time

As our family's official vacation planner, I've found that half the joy of traveling is found in the anticipation. Choosing where to go, when to go, and what to do once we get there is almost as much fun as actually going there. Unfortunately, it's easy for the busyness of life to crowd out our vacation time. So make a plan and get on the path to seeing a new part of the world.

Note some places you want to visit in the year ahead—and put them on your calendar.

The LORD replied, "I will personally go with you, Moses, and I will give you rest—everything will be fine for you." — EXODUS 33:14

Daring to *Dream*

We limit our dreams because all we can see are the obstacles to achieving them. There usually are legitimate barriers to what we wish we could do. But sometimes God is calling us to things we could never imagine, and we won't see that if we don't let ourselves dream a little. This is one of those times when there are no dreams too big and no bad ideas.

List the things you would love to accomplish if you were not limited by time, fear, or circumstances. Is there something on that list that you could actually do if you put your mind to it?

_____

_____

_____

_____

_____

_____

_____

_____

_____

_____

Unless the LORD builds a house, the work of the builders is wasted.
Unless the LORD protects a city, guarding it with sentries will do no good.
— PSALM 127:1

Loving Others

We all have people who are a little prickly, a little hard to love, a little bit of a challenge to get along with. These relationships require more effort on our part. This week, instead of seeing these people as a challenge, try to view them as an opportunity to let Christ's love flow through you.

Make a list of some difficult people in your life, and next to each one write down something kind you can do for them in the week ahead.

Don't look out only for your own interests, but take an interest in others, too.
— PHILIPPIANS 2:4

Books to Read

Some years I make a reading goal—a specific number of books I'd like to read during the months ahead. I find that when I have a goal or a reading list or a pile of books next to my bed, I'm more likely to reach for a book instead of scrolling through my newsfeed. Ask your friends for some recommendations and make a plan to explore some new literature.

Which books would you like to read in the next few months?

Wise words are like deep waters; wisdom flows from the wise like a bubbling brook. — PROVERBS 18:4

Being a Friend

Each of us has seasons of loneliness, times when circumstances prevent us from having the kind of deep, life-giving relationships we long for. The best way to pull ourselves out of those seasons and the self-pity that often accompanies them is to be a friend. Solve someone else's loneliness problem and you'll find that you solved your own as well.

Are there people in your life who seem lonely? How can you reach out to them?

_____

_____

_____

_____

_____

_____

_____

_____

_____

Father to the fatherless, defender of widows—this is God, whose dwelling is holy. God places the lonely in families; he sets the prisoners free and gives them joy. —PSALM 68:5-6

The Lord is my strength and my song.

PSALM 118:14

More of These

It's not hard to find things to complain about. Our expectations and hopes rarely match reality. But complaining only brings our mood down and doesn't solve anything anyway. A better strategy is to figure out what we want more of, and then add those things. I want more friends, more rest, more family dinners. What do you want more of?

Write down some things you want more of in your life.

_____

_____

_____

_____

_____

_____

What do you benefit if you gain the whole world but lose your own soul?
— MARK 8:36

Less of These

Professional organizers tell us that we can have a much more calm and productive life if we clear out the clutter. Just fifteen minutes a day of getting rid of things that no longer serve us well can improve our mood and make our home a more welcoming place. Carry that concept beyond your possessions and think of what is cluttering up your life in all areas—heart, mind, and body.

List some things you want less of in your life.

_____

_____

_____

_____

_____

_____

_____

_____

_____

_____

_____

Throw off your old sinful nature and your former way of life, which is corrupted by lust and deception. Instead, let the Spirit renew your thoughts and attitudes.
— EPHESIANS 4:22-23

The Perfect Life

It is great to appreciate all the wonderful blessings in our lives and be content with where God has us. Sometimes it's also helpful to ask ourselves whether God wants to take us somewhere else. What is your perfect life? Maybe it's the one you're living, maybe there are some new goals God wants you to make, or maybe it's a combination of the two.

If money, time, and life circumstances were no obstacle, what would be your perfect life?

The LORD's plans stand firm forever; his intentions can never be shaken.
— PSALM 33:11

Goals
for the Month

Our calendars and to-do lists get filled with urgent things. We are so busy with what needs to get done in the next day or two that sometimes we can't see beyond that. Here is some space to step back and get a bigger-picture view of what you want to accomplish. What are the big goals you need to achieve in the next month?

Think about your top three goals for the month ahead. Do you have a strategy to meet those goals?

_____

_____

_____

_____

_____

_____

_____

_____

_____

And this same God who takes care of me will supply all your needs from his glorious riches, which have been given to us in Christ Jesus. — PHILIPPIANS 4:19

Goals
for the Year

Zoom out a little further than your monthly goals—what do you want to do in the next year? You might think in terms of a goal for your body, a goal for your mind, and a goal for your spiritual life. Then break it down into steps and put monthly goals in your calendar so you'll actually accomplish it.

List the top three goals you'd like to accomplish in the year ahead. Do you have a strategy to meet those goals?

Commit your actions to the LORD, and your plans will succeed.
— PROVERBS 16:3

"Peace I leave with you; My peace I give to you."

JOHN 14:27

God's Amazing
Attributes

Every page of God's Word shows us a new precious treasure of who He is. Even if we worship Him for our entire lifetime and beyond, we will never get to the end of all the glorious things we can praise Him for. Yet we often fail to think about those things. Here's your space to worship God for who He is.

Write down some of the things you praise God for—His amazing attributes.

Jesus Christ is the same yesterday, today, and forever. — HEBREWS 13:8

Give Thanks
to the Lord

Whether your life right now is full of celebration or sorrow, whether you are in the heights of joy or the depths of despair, you have something to be thankful for. God is always faithful, and each day He demonstrates His love to you. Celebrate and appreciate all the things you have to be thankful for by writing them down.

List the things you are thankful for—what God has done for you.

_____

_____

_____

_____

_____

_____

_____

_____

_____

_____

Give thanks to the Lord, for he is good! His faithful love endures forever.
—1 CHRONICLES 16:34

Praying for
Loved Ones

Too often my prayers are reduced to "bless Mary" or "heal Tom." Life is busy and, if we're honest, prayer can feel monotonous. Rejuvenate your prayer life by praying deeply for someone you love. Don't settle for generalizations; think about all the blessings you want to see God bring into their lives and boldly ask for those things.

Choose someone you love and write down the prayers you have for them.

Pray in the Spirit at all times and on every occasion. Stay alert and be persistent in your prayers for all believers everywhere. — EPHESIANS 6:18

Praying for *Yourself*

The last list was about deep, specific prayers for someone you love. Now it's your turn—think about what you need more of in your life, what you long to see God do, what you most need and want from Him. Don't hold back; ask God to do big things in your life so you can display His glory and share His love with others.

Write down some bold prayers you have for yourself in the year ahead.

"But if you remain in me and my words remain in you, you may ask for anything you want, and it will be granted!" — JOHN 15:7

Praying about Burdens

The older I get, the more trouble I have sleeping. I run through conversations in my mind of things I wish I had said or wish I hadn't said. I worry about my loved ones and the burdens I carry for them. I worry about my own burdens. God invites us to hand all those things over to Him and rest in His care.

List the burdens you are carrying, the things that you think about at night when you can't sleep. Then ask God to give you His peace about those things, either by giving you wisdom for how to solve them or a sense of surrender to His will.

Give all your worries and cares to God, for He cares about you. — 1 PETER 5:7

In
everything
give
thanks.

1 THESSALONIANS 5:18

Celebrating
Loved Ones

If you were to put all your favorite people in a room together, who would be there? God has given you friends and family to enjoy life with, to share the joy and divide the sorrow. Celebrate all those relationships by reminding yourself of these precious gifts from God.

List the people who make you happy—and thank God for them!

_____

_____

_____

_____

_____

_____

_____

_____

_____

_____

_____

Every time I think of you, I give thanks to my God. — PHILIPPIANS 1:3

Confessing
Negativity

Grumbling. Arguing. Complaining. They are unpleasant to be around, and they are all symptoms of a bad attitude. But although these negative attitudes are easy to spot in others, we often become blinded to them in ourselves. Think about your words and behavior over the last few days and identify the nasty attitudes you need to banish from your heart.

Which negative attitudes do you need to prune from your life? Ask God to help you do that.

Do everything without complaining and arguing. — PHILIPPIANS 2:14

Healthy
Heart Habits

The last journal entry helped you identify the negative attitudes you need to cut out of your life. Now it's time to think about the heart attitudes you'd like to put on. What kinds of heart habits and fruits of the Spirit do you think God wants to grow in you? What does He want to clothe you with?

Reflect on some positive attitudes you need to put on—and ask God to help you do that.

_____

_____

_____

_____

_____

_____

_____

_____

_____

_____

Since God chose you to be the holy people he loves, you must clothe yourselves with tenderhearted mercy, kindness, humility, gentleness, and patience.
— COLOSSIANS 3:12

Praying for *Leaders*

The Bible reminds us to respect those in authority over us and to obey them as an act of obedience to God. That can be difficult, especially if we don't agree with their decisions. The first step is to pray for them. If you think about it, praying for wisdom for our leaders is a way of praying for ourselves, since their decisions directly affect us and our communities.

List those who are in leadership over you, and prayers you have for them.

_____

_____

_____

_____

_____

_____

_____

_____

_____

_____

I urge you, first of all, to pray for all people. Ask God to help them; intercede on their behalf, and give thanks for them. — 1 TIMOTHY 2:1

Interceding for Others

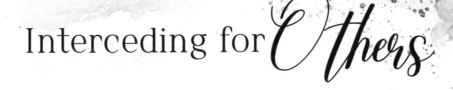

Giving to organizations and causes we believe in is one way to support them and further their effectiveness. But even more crucial for their ministry is our prayers. Be specific and strategic in the way you intercede for God's work in your community and around the world. "The earnest prayer of a righteous person has great power and produces wonderful results" (James 5:16).

Which organizations and causes are close to your heart? Pray for them.

Dear friend, I hope all is well with you and that you are as healthy in body as you are strong in spirit. — 3 JOHN 1:2

He has made everything beautiful in its time.

ECCLESIASTES 3:11

Praying for Your
Church Family

Your pastor and church staff face opposition and challenges you can't even imagine. In addition to the letters and comments from disgruntled congregants they receive each week, they experience intense spiritual warfare as they preach and minister in Jesus' name. Pray specifically for them and their families, and send an encouraging note to let them know you're praying for them.

List your church pastors and staff members and a specific prayer you have for each of them.

_____

_____

_____

_____

_____

_____

_____

_____

I pray that your hearts will be flooded with light so that you can understand the confident hope he has given to those he called—his holy people who are his rich and glorious inheritance. — EPHESIANS 1:18

Regrets and *Forgiveness*

We carry around regrets like a burden on our backs, rehashing the wrongs we've done as a way to atone for them. God doesn't want that for us. He died to forgive us and release us from the pain of past sin. Leave all those regrets here, receive God's forgiveness, and move forward in freedom, unencumbered by regret.

What are some regrets you have? Confess the part your sin played in those things, and then claim God's forgiveness for those things.

_____

_____

_____

_____

_____

_____

_____

_____

_____

_____

_____

If we confess our sins to him, he is faithful and just to forgive us our sins and to cleanse us from all wickedness. — 1 JOHN 1:9

Praying Scripture

Praying God's words back to Him is a powerful way to interact with Scripture and deepen our understanding of God's heart. Scripture can provide a blueprint for prayer, beginning with specific prayers like the Lord's Prayer and going far beyond as we pray psalms and other passages. There is no better way to pray than to meditate on God's Word and turn it into prayer.

List your favorite verses to pray and pray them for yourself and those you love.

_____

_____

_____

_____

_____

_____

_____

_____

_____

_____

I cried out to the LORD, and he answered me from his holy mountain.
— PSALM 3:4

Praying for Faith

Faith as small as a mustard seed can move mountains (Matthew 17:20). I think for the most part our faith—and our prayers—are far too small. We don't believe God can really fix what is broken, whether it is bodies or families or dreams. But God can do what seems impossible, and He will do everything that is in His perfect will. Our job is to believe.

Reflect on some things you struggle to believe God for, and ask Him to grow your faith.

_____

_____

_____

_____

_____

_____

_____

It is impossible to please God without faith. Anyone who wants to come to him must believe that God exists and that he rewards those who sincerely seek him.
— HEBREWS 11:6

Confessing Fear

Sometimes naming our fears strips them of their power. Seeing them written down in ink helps us to see that many of them are unlikely to happen, and all of them can be faced with the strength God provides. Write down the things that seem scary and watch them fade in the light of God's loving-kindness.

List some things you're afraid of and ask God to give you courage.

The LORD is my light and my salvation—so why should I be afraid? The LORD is my fortress, protecting me from danger, so why should I tremble?
— PSALM 27:1

Let all that you do be done in love.

1 CORINTHIANS 16:14

Blessings
for Others

God loves to pour out blessings on His children. Ephesians 1:3 says He has "blessed us with every spiritual blessing in the heavenly realms because we are united with Christ," and then lists some of those blessings—culminating in the kindness, wisdom, and understanding He showers on us. Ponder all the spiritual blessings listed in Scripture and write out a prayer that God will bless someone you love in those ways.

Think of someone close to you and write down the blessings you desire for them.

_____

_____

_____

_____

_____

_____

_____

_____

_____

We are confident that he hears us whenever we ask for anything that pleases him. — 1 JOHN 5:14

Becoming like Jesus

Jesus told us to take up our cross and follow Him (Luke 9:23), and Paul told us to imitate Him in the same way a child imitates her father (Ephesians 5:1). The only way to do that is to become His student, devoting ourselves to learning what God is like. Study God's attributes in His Word and strive to become more like Him.

Which attributes of God do you need more of in your life? Ask Him for more of Himself.

Don't copy the behavior and customs of this world, but let God transform you into a new person by changing the way you think. — ROMANS 12:2

Praying for

Self-Control

We set our goals and make our resolutions and set up systems to achieve them. We start out with a lot of optimism and the best of intentions. But then old habits creep in, and before we know it, we have given up. The best way to combat this slow loss of self-discipline is to identify our areas of struggle and ask for God's help to do what is right.

In which areas do you find it difficult to have self-control? Ask God to help you.

_____

_____

_____

_____

_____

_____

_____

_____

_____

_____

The temptations in your life are no different from what others experience. And God is faithful. He will not allow the temptation to be more than you can stand. When you are tempted, he will show you a way out so that you can endure. — 1 CORINTHIANS 10:13

Future Plans

None of us can see into the future—God chooses to keep that a secret—but we can make a few predictions about what we think is coming in the next year. And we can dream. Looking at the year ahead, what dreams is God planting in your heart? Where does He seem to be taking you?

List the dreams you have for the year ahead, and then pray about them. Is God calling you to pursue one or more of them?

_____

_____

_____

_____

_____

_____

_____

_____

_____

But those who trust in the LORD will find new strength. They will soar high on wings like eagles. They will run and not grow weary. They will walk and not faint. — ISAIAH 40:31

God's Plans

Our culture tells us to dream our dreams and set our goals, but far better is to identify God's goals for us. He leads us on paths of peace and righteousness. Think about all areas of your life—spiritual and physical—and write down the goals God seems to be leading you toward. Set aside your own goals and pursue His instead.

Write down the goals you think God has for you.

Therefore, let us offer through Jesus a continual sacrifice of praise to God, proclaiming our allegiance to his name. — HEBREWS 13:15

"With God all things are possible."

MATTHEW 19:26

Learning through
Frustration

As emotions go, frustration often feels a little useless. It makes us feel stagnant. Sometimes, however, frustration is the catalyst for positive change. There is a type of holy frustration that leads us to root out sin and pursue righteousness or to move out of a job that doesn't fit us anymore into a place we can be more fruitful. Identify your frustrations and then decide whether you should set them aside or take action.

List the things that are frustrating you right now and ask God for His perspective on those things. What is He teaching you?

And we know that God causes everything to work together for the good of those who love God and are called according to his purpose for them.
— ROMANS 8:28

Waiting on the Lord

None of us likes to wait. We don't mind resting or relaxing, but waiting implies impatience and an eagerness to get to the next thing. We want what we want, and we want it now. But God often keeps us in the waiting room because it is there that we learn patience, rest, and trust. Waiting on God is never wasted time, it's part of the process.

What are you waiting for right now? Ask God for patience.

_____

_____

_____

_____

_____

_____

_____

_____

Even though the fig trees have no blossoms, and there are no grapes on the vines . . . yet I will rejoice in the Lord! I will be joyful in the God of my salvation!
— HABAKKUK 3:17-18

Called to Love

The people we love the most or work closely with can be the most aggravating. They know how to push our buttons, and when they hurt us the hurt goes deep. Those times when we are really struggling with someone are the times we are called to love them the best—and that starts by praying specific and big prayers for them.

List some people you are having a hard time loving right now, and write out some prayers for each of them.

"I am giving you a new commandment: Love each other. Just as I have loved you, you should love each other." — JOHN 13:34

Looking to Eternity

For the Christian, our true, ultimate hope lies in the fact that we will spend eternity with God. That is what we are living for and looking forward to. That is what enables us to face life with joy even when we pass through the shadow of death. Think about all the promises God has made about heaven and make them concrete and real by writing them down.

Reflect on some things you're looking forward to about heaven.

_____

_____

_____

_____

_____

_____

_____

_____

_____

_____

He will wipe every tear from their eyes, and there will be no more death or sorrow or crying or pain. All these things are gone forever. — REVELATION 21:4

Lessons Learned

God never leaves us where we are. He is always working to transform and redeem and make us into the people He created us to be. The best life is found in working with Him to learn the lessons He's trying to teach. Praise God for all the lessons He's taught you this year, even the painful ones.

List some lessons God has taught you this year, and thank Him for them.

O God, you have taught me from my earliest childhood, and I constantly tell others about the wonderful things you do. — PSALM 71:17

Blessed is the one who trusts in the Lord.

JEREMIAH 17:7